MACHINE

LEARNING

Author: John Slavio

TABLE OF CONTENTS

DISCLAIMER

ABOUT THE AUTHOR

John Slavio is a programmer who is passionate about the reach of the internet and the interaction of the internet with daily devices. He has automated several home devices to make them 'smart' and connect them to high speed internet. His passions involve computer security, iOT, hardware programming and blogging.

WHAT IS MACHINE LEARNING?

To understand what machine learning is and how it's important to our everyday lives, you first have to go over what programming is and how machine-learning relates to it. In programming, everything is sequential, meaning that once one command from line 1 is completed then the program goes on to the next line to carry out the next command. However, due to how information is saved within a computer, we have temporary access to previous information that can then be changed and the subsequent information that is based on that information is changed after that.

This is due to something called a Memory Reference, which is assigned to any information inside of the computer. You can think of a memory reference as a location of a house inside of a neighborhood. Therefore, you can tell your driver to go down a neighborhood of addresses and then, once you see the house you're looking for, you can have them perform a U-turn so that you can arrive at the address that you were trying to get to. This is conceptually similar to how an Unordered Array Sort works inside of programming. There have been many methods of making such a path such as the infamous GOTO method from the early days of programming to the more modern methods of running Loops and Recursion.

Machine learning doesn't work without a loop or a method of recursion because machine learning is the machine finding a successful result, storing it, and then rerunning the program so that it further refines what it finds as a successful result. This allows the machine to not only optimize the path towards getting that successful result but also for it to "learn" how to do something. Therefore, machine learning can be described as a machine going to a specific address several times but each time that it is set to go to that address, it remembers how it got there in the first place and searches for more optimal paths to get there faster.

Let's walk through a scenario so that you can get a better grasp of what I mean by this because this can be a very confusing topic to discuss no matter what level you are at with programming. Imagine that you purchased a brand-new game and you have no idea how to play it. You also bought a new console that has buttons that you have never played with before. The very first time that you boot up the game, you need to learn all the new moves but the game that you bought doesn't included a tutorial so you just have to continually press buttons to figure out what things do. You are, however, handed a single goal that you must accomplish by the time you get to the end of the level. Therefore, you spend a small amount of time or even large amount of time just figuring out how everything moves in the current space that you've been given. Once you understand, on the most basic level, how these buttons work you begin to push yourself towards the goal but the second you die you have to start out at the beginning. As a human being, you remember everything you did beforehand in order to figure out how the buttons worked. Your measure of success is how far you get towards that goal. You then begin to work your way towards the goal and continue to die and make mistakes until you finally manage to accomplish that goal.

This is essentially what machine learning is doing, but with a few key differences. The first difference is that the computer doesn't even know how games work. That, in it of itself, is bizarre and extremely hard to conceptualize since it involves not knowing something that's been around with you since, probably, birth. However, it is given certain functions that it can utilize in order to go further in the game but it doesn't know what those functions will do for it and how to utilize those functions to the best degree. Even worse, the control schema is usually un-made for the program. In other words, not only is the computer usually not handed the controller with buttons but it doesn't even know that buttons exist. It has to first create the controller in order to do anything in the first place. Therefore, it knows that the rules of its' program say that it's required to move in a specific direction and that it has to accomplish a goal. It has to create a system for it to move and since it knows that there is a rule about X and Y when it comes to movement on the screen, it develops calculations that will help it move on the screen. Once it remembers how to create those from scratch by placing the information in the save file, it can then begin to move on the screen but it still doesn't know what the best direction is. Therefore, it will move in one direction until it figures out that it needs to move in multiple directions. Once it figures out that it needs to multiply the amount of directions that it moves in, it then begins to test different movement paths in order to optimize what it knows at the current time. Some movements will seem like an optimization, for the human being that is watching the machine learning taking place, but sometimes the computer believes that the action didn't result in the appropriate outcome. Therefore, sometimes when the computer has moved exceedingly far but gets a false negative result, it will revert back to a previous stage in order to further optimize where it is going. This is just how the machine learning begins in a machine learning environment and this is only one case where machine learning has been applied before; simply so that other people can conceptualize what machine learning does. This also represents one particular type of machine learning called unsupervised machine learning, which simply means that the program will continue to do something until it fails and then once it fails it will utilize all the data that it has gathered to optimize and further its goals towards accomplishing the one goal that you handed it. However, there are several different forms of learning for machines because humans handle things differently.

One great example is the English grammar that we speak with, which has a lot of rules. There are so many rules in English when it comes to the proper grammar that the average person does not know all of their appropriate grammar rules but there are multiple versions of English. To make things even worse for the machine, English contains something called context. For instance, a popular idiom that is currently used in society is the term "Netflix and chill" and this term has several different meanings depending on the context. If your parent asks you if you want to just watch some Netflix and chill, then you take it as a sign that you and your parents will be hanging out while watching Netflix. However, if your significant other says that they want to Netflix and chill, that usually means that someone is going to get laid that night. Finally, if you text your friend that you're going to Netflix and chill then that simply means that you're going to sit down and watch Netflix while chilling out wherever you sit or lay. There were three separate meanings for the same idiom and the computer has to figure out what each one means based on only the definitions set forth by the people who gave them the definitions, which is not always the institution for grammar or the dictionary. This presents a huge problem for machines but shows a great area for applications since most people simply can't keep up with the sheer number of rules that it takes to master the English language.

IMPORTANCE OF MACHINE LEARNING / APPLICATIONS

There are several different applications for machine learning and all of them are useful to our everyday lives because of how our everyday lives are run. The problem with machine learning is that you often have to convince people who don't understand computer science on a level that's needed in order to understand how useful machine learning is. The average individual does not need more than one language and usually doesn't need anything that requires complex abstraction. This becomes a problem whenever you are trying to fundraise for a more advanced version of machine learning. This is why you see massive companies supporting smaller companies. Machine learning doesn't take that much in terms of raw power because you can run machine learning on a single-core processor without ever experiencing any problems with the machine. A lot of people think that they need a supercomputer for machine learning because the people who are currently researching machine learning in the open public media space often display enormous machines that are specifically for machine learning.

However, you have to understand that machine learning is just code and it will run as fast as you've written it based on the hardware that is available to it. As an example, you can utilize the standard Raspberry Pi 3 with its quad-core processor and run a quad-core machine learning algorithm. This will be nowhere near as fast as the enormous complex that Google has built for their machine learning algorithms but it will still run because you have given it a processor that it can use in order to run logic. You don't need a complex set up in order to achieve machine learning, but it will make it much faster. This is because you need more than one core in order to have something called a neural network. A neural network can either be virtual or real, which means that the neural network is either using simulated processors or it's using real processors. The difference between a simulated processor and a real processor is that a simulated processor will usually run slower, it takes a lot more to set up a simulated processor, and most of the time the real processor will be much more reliable when it comes to raw data processing. However, many people use simulator processing in order to get started with machine learning because it's an easy and affordable way to learn how machine learning works. Let's go over some of the immediate applications that machine learning can greatly affect and improve.

The Law

One of the great things about machine learning is that it teaches machines one aspect of the human nature that has previously been untouched. What I'm talking about here is it teaches the context of a situation. You may have heard of the recent lawyer that is actually an artificial intelligence machine. This was one of the very first achievements for machine learning. This new lawyer was hired by law firm to handle certain types of cases. A lot of people think that the machine might mess up and this is possible if the researchers and Law Firms behind this artificial intelligence don't implement the machine learning in the correct process. This new machine is responsible for learning all the laws and law cases within its given area of expertise. This machine is handed the entire Library available to all lawyers so that it can use the machine learning algorithm that it has been programmed with to study these different cases. This means that the robot has to conceptualize the context of the law to show that it understands where that law can be applied and where that law just doesn't make sense. This shows off a great example of where machine learning can be applied and thus improve the industry by existing in that industry. The average lawyer will have to commit hundreds of hours of research on a single difficult case in order to provide an unsure application inside of the courtroom. On the other hand, the robot will not need to wait around for anything because it has direct access to all of the previous cases dealing with that specific industry of law and so it is able to pull up that information as it needs it. This would result in more wins for the defendant or prosecutor, depending on who used A.I.

Machine Generated Games

Have you ever noticed that the games that we make are a lot shorter than the games of the previous generation? Let's think about Legend of Zelda, the original. This game was hours long and is considered a classic amongst games. In fact, The Legend of Zelda series has often been extremely long compared to other games in its generation. However, that doesn't mean that the game is always that long because, in reality, the newer games have often had a very short main story while having multiple side stories to help extend the amount of time that it takes to get through the main story. This is very different compared to the previous games inside of the Legend of Zelda series. In the very first Legend of Zelda series, there were almost no side quests. However, in the newest generation of game inside of the Legend of Zelda series you have hundreds of side quests that you need to complete in order to get better items to complete the main story. This is not because the writers of the Legend of Zelda series are incapable of writing a longer story. Instead, video games have gotten so complex that it takes years to write a short story. You have to also take into account all the land that is generated onto the screen along with character models, building models, cinematic scenes, and even the physics behind each and every one of the characters moves. As we've gotten better at making graphically good-looking games, we've gotten worse in the amount of time that it takes to make those games. It's understandable and completely forgivable because it's the difference between making a crayon drawing of stick figures vs the Mona Lisa with thousand-dollar paint sticks. However, machine learning has the ability to fix this problem. Instead of dealing with games that are extremely short or games that are extremely buggy, you can have a machine learning algorithm develop a game that will be generally liked by the public. The machine can auto generate the type of land needed for the game, which saves hundreds of hours. The animations for character model movements can be handed parameters and auto generate the needed algorithms for the animations, which would save even more hundreds of hours. It can even auto generate enemies based on enemy sketches, which would leave the story and direction of the game up to the creators.

Language Translation

One aspect that we've already talked about is having a machine learn a language and we already know just how complicated it is for machine to learn English in all of its various forms. However, English isn't the only language on this planet and there are so many languages on the

18

planet that no one knows them all. In fact, many people spend their entire lives simply studying different languages so that they can interpret languages for others. A machine, on the other hand, can learn all of the languages, provided that we have enough space to store all the language rules and then enough space to store all the context that the language might be in. Google is already doing this and every time that you use voice typing or the Google auto word feature, you add to the data set that the Google learning machine is currently using. If one were to travel back to when Google was first predicting the words that someone would use, they would find that the predictions were usually only halfway correct and even laughable at sometimes. This was because the data set that the learning machine was using was not as comprehensive as it is today. Today, some writers are switching to voice typing over regular typing because not only can they speak faster than they can type but the machine is really good at predicting the words that they speak along with the words inside of the context. A common trend that you will see if you ever use voice type is that the machine will utilize a word immediately to see if that's the correct word and once a sentence has been completed or the person has stopped talking, the machine will go back over the information and try to predict the context that the author is speaking in. Let me tell you right now, this method of typing is nowhere near accurate but it has gotten better with time. As more and more authors utilize voice typing, they find that the predictions are clearer and more precise. This is because the author is usually contributing to the library that the machine learning is using as they use the library.

More Advanced Electronics

As of right now, there is a hidden curtain for most people when it comes to the GPU and the CPU. A lot of people think that the year in which the GPU was released was also the year in which it was conceived or it was conceived in the prior year. The truth of the matter is that it almost takes a decade for the company to generate a GPU or CPU. It takes thousands to millions of hours in order to lay down the architecture that it takes to just make the chip follow all logical paths. We are talking about a chip that houses billions if not trillions of different pathways that it can utilize so that it is made quicker than the previous chip. There is no human made way to reduce the amount of time that it takes to generate a GPU and a CPU. All of the pathways that it takes in order to improve upon a chip that was previously fast in order to make it faster takes a mathematician, a mechanic, and a slew of other fields filled with thousands of people working on tiny parts of their own section. The creation of a CPU and a GPU are marvelous wonders that only a few get to experience. The average person just sees a tiny square that they fit into their motherboard. They don't realize just how complex the architecture underneath it really is and how many man-hours it went into in order for that GPU or CPU to be created.

If a computer is taught how these CPUs and GPUs are made, then you have the possibility that the learning algorithm that was used would be able to create a better and more sophisticated GPU and CPU architecture. The only problem with this is that we make brakes and advances in science by turning to unsuspecting sources. It was only a couple of decades ago when we were using the cathode tube in order to do our calculations and it took a weird and bizarre action in order to switch to the current transistors that we use today. As of right now, the only upgrade from the normal transistors inside of the GPU and CPU is a quantum CPU, which takes billions of dollars in order to generate just a couple of them. If it wasn't for the investments that google and many other giant computer-based companies were willing to make towards the advancement of the quantum CPU, quantum CPUs would never exist. However, a learning algorithm can optimize the speed at which the current variables allow us to go. As of right now, humans are limited in their methods of not only mathematics and vision but also the inability to see unforeseen consequences. A great example of this is the current HBM technology that was released by AMD. The invention of HBM is marvelous but due to the unforeseen consequences, the CPU and GPU that currently use this technology are underused because they did not foresee that their driver support would bottleneck the capabilities of their invention. A machine learning algorithm would have taken in driver support as a factor and would have developed an appropriate driver for the already known motherboards that would be supporting the new AMD CPUs.

Introduction to Statistics for Machine Learning

When people talk about statistics gained from machine learning you will almost never see direct statistics. What I mean by this is you will almost always see trends of Statistics rather than direct numbers. It's a little hard to wrap your head around this, but imagine if you were to look at a graph of individuals who lived in a specific area. Direct statistics would be how many people lived in each house, the general consensus of the specific area, and the average age of the house owner. These are statistics that can be programmed and don't need any type of machine learning. Programmers hate wasting resources and so they tend to only use machine learning if it's a problem that is so large or complex that it requires machine learning. Let's talk about that specific area of living again in order to show you an example of this. Say that you were trying to find the perfect individual to advertise to because you have a house in this area and you want to sell it. By looking at the ages of all the people who own houses in the neighborhood, you are not likely to gain anything other than a weird mixture of different numbers because people of all ages own houses and it's very rare that an entire neighborhood is filled with the same generation of age. Instead, machine-learning would allow you to grab all those ages and figure out a trend of those ages. It would show you that there are more senior individuals living in the area than younger individuals or there are more single parents living in the area then married couples. You may not think that such a trend would be important, but a homeowner is usually looking for not only a house that they're comfortable living in but also a neighborhood that they think they can get along with. Not everyone can be as shut-in as some developers and other professions, which means that they're likely going to go outside and try to meet the neighbors if they can. This is especially true of older generations since they were born before the times where everybody was scared to go outside in the first place.

By utilizing the machine learning, you're able to gain a better access to the view of the people living in that area. Not only does this give you access to the trends of the people living in that area, it gives you questions that you need to answer such as why those specific people are living in that area. By gathering further data in order to help you understand the situation, which means that you would go door-to-door to ask for a questionnaire to be filled out you automatically fill out all the parts that you need in order to advertise that house to someone who is more likely to buy it. Machine learning is more about predictions then it is about current times, which is why it is often either considered a hobby activity, a new fringe science activity, and even a global activity. These are all jobs where the idea is to tinker with it to see what's possible. It's not about the real-world applications up front but rather the real-world applications that could be applied later down the road. Let's say we were to go looking for areas that would have a predictability to it. Something that is easily predictable is how many people will buy a specific price range of phones.

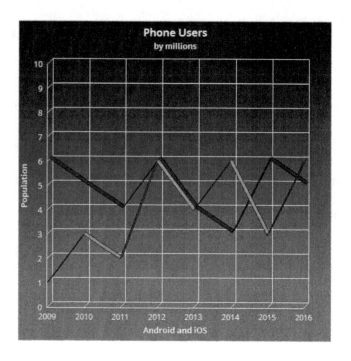

In this graph, we would easily be able to see that both Android and iOS have had rigorous competition with each other over the years. This graph isn't actually real, but one could easily see a steady trend that the users tend to be opposite of each other most of the time. However, what is different with machine learning is that it would be able to predict that after every other Android release the user base increases but iOS only increases after every second release. This would be incredibly useful to those who have to decide what device to show advertisements on more. While this graph may be simple, it could easily be expanded to include all the different Android phones along with determining the updating patterns and current common version of Android. As an Android developer, understanding what version of Android is available for me to develop on and how often they update is absolutely vital for not only creating Android applications but also maintaining them. Being able to predict future updates and when users might be switching to new phones also helps companies determine when to provide platforms more support. As you can see, being able to predict future trends based on current data trends means that machine learning can be useful for smartphones to individuals working in artistry, programming, marketing, customer service, engineers, and even banking. What, you didn't see that? An application needs an artist, a programmer, and even an engineer to be a top-class application in most cases. When those applications have problems, they need more programmers, individuals at customer service, and, sometimes, banking individuals. To manage the business those applications run on, you need all the services that would come with banking such as bookkeeping.

Better predictions mean that more people have the opportunity to work and the cycle increases.

INTRODUCTION TO STATISTICS FOR MACHINE LEARNING

Alright so let's begin breaking down a basic machine learning algorithm so that you can wrap your head around this and get full flung into it. The problem with machine learning for the average programmer is that the beginning steps often seem like you're just writing a program like you normally would, but there's some key differences between a normal control flow in a development environment and a control flow in a machine learning environment.

Features

In order to begin learning machine learning, you first have to understand what a feature is. If you go look at a mirror, you will see that you have several different features. You have hair, nose, eyes, and even a mouth out of which to eat. These are basic and general features of nearly every creature on the planet. The trick with what I just said was that you likely thought of the fish who do not inherit hair and this is true, but this also what represents the difference between features and why they are important. You just performed the very first decision that nearly every machine would make if they had to determine if the animal lived on the ground or in the ocean. Then you likely went and said that bacteria don't have mouths, which is also true and another decision that a machine would make in order to determine if the creature was a bacterium or not. These features determine where the machine learning will go when you hand it data to work with. As an example, I set up an array inside of JavaScript to show you what a feature might look like if we were trying to utilize data to say that it was red or it was blue. This could be a true or false, but it could also represent a true in that blue is darker than red and that red is lighter than blue.

```
var redOrBlue = [0,1,0,1,1,0,1,0,0,1,0,1,0,1]
```

When you think of features, you have to think of something unique or that's different from all of the other forms of data that you have. For instance, whenever they do statistics on races inside of school they will often choose the race of the person rather than the nationality because an individual may be an American and be Caucasian but could also be African-American, Hispanic, or Asian etc. The researchers might also decide to separate those who were born in America separate from those who were born outside of America so that they get a more refined view of their data. The color and nationality, in this instance, represents two unique features that cannot be faked and are different from the other sets of data. For humans, it helps us separate the individuals so that we can make sense of the numbers while, for machines, it helps to improve the level of predictability of future students that might be going to the school. This is why features are extremely important and why you always need to make sure that they fit at least two of three of the following parameters.

- Is this feature common amongst all of the data set?

- Does this feature only represent a small portion of the data set?

- Is the feature representative of a consistent trait?

We first want to make sure that the feature that we choose is going to be something that we see throughout the data set. Once we make sure that this is common enough for us to use, we also want to make sure that it isn't shared amongst every other thing inside of the data set or else the feature becomes pointless. Lastly, we want to make sure that the event or character trait or feature is consistent rather than random because if the feature is random then it doesn't help us increase the predictability of the end result. This is similar to saying that all books have written material, but only one of them is written in Alien. No one is going to find that one book written by an alien easy to predict when they're trying to search through books.

The Decision Tree

Let's go ahead and continue with our college example in order to explain the decision tree. A decision tree is a map of decisions that a machine will have to go through in order to determine the final result. I'm going to use 3 variables, generated automatically with the following code:

```
var ethnicityArray = [];
var origins = [];
var fieldOfStudy = [];

for(var i = 0; i <= 10; i++){
 ethnicityArray[i] = Math.round((Math.random() *
10) + 1);
 origins[i] = (Math.random()*2) <= 1 ? 1 : 2
 var fiveDenominator =
(Math.round((Math.random()*10 + 1)))
 fieldOfStudy[i] = fiveDenominator < 5?
fiveDenominator : fiveDenominator - 5
}
```

This will help determine the decision tree of a very basic algorithm. This means that there will be a possibility of ten ethnicities, two origins, and six fields of study for a group of 10 people. In other words, it gives you the below dataset to work with (if you run it, it is random so you are likely not going to get the same numbers as me but this does not matter):

```
var ethnicityArray = [7,6,9,10,3,10,5,6,2,5,9]
var origins = [2,2,1,2,1,1,1,2,1,1,1]
var fieldOfStudy = [6,1,3,1,2,3,4,1,2,3,3]
```

Now that we know our inputs, we can look at what is called a decision tree.

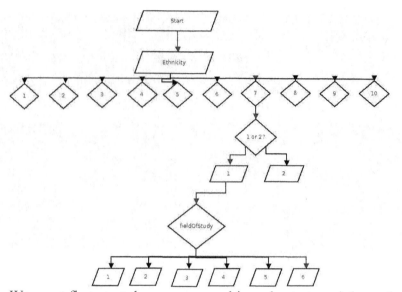

We must first start the program and in order to travel the path of one outcome, we have to follow six different paths. According to the rule of Combinations, we have ten choices that can each turn into two results, and this can then turn into six more results each.

$$(6^2)2 = 72$$

That is how many possible outcomes could have occurred at the beginning of the Decision Tree. The computer puts in ethnicity to start the categorization process, we then provide it with the input of seven. The next decision is to see if it is a 1 or a 2. We hand it a 1 so that it can make the next decision. Now that it asks what the field of study is, we

34

hand it a 6. That's all good and dandy, but what does this actually accomplish? Any programmer could write a Decision Tree and not need machine learning to do this, so why would we need machine learning for this? Perhaps we are attempting to predict who the next student is, where they come from, and what field of study they are likely to join so that we can plan a budget based on how likely a student is to go into that field of study along with special programs other studies might need to boost their numbers.

Once again, we do not need to have machine learning perform such a calculation because all we would need to do is write an algorithm that calculates the percentage of ethnicity, origin, and field of study to provide us with the bigger numbers. The key here, the part I'm trying to get you to say is "I don't know" because that's the exact reason why you would need machine learning. In all of the steps during this Decision Tree, the computer has been handed exact numbers and has never had to fill in the gaps. Let's say that we don't know the next student in our data set and we want the machine to predict the next student.

Your First Hello World Machine Learning Algorithm

Now, I want you to keep in mind that we are working with a very limited scope when it comes to machine learning. This will be a Hello World of sorts for machine learning. Let's first write what we would use in order to predict the outcome of the next student.

```
var ethnicityArray = [7,6,9,10,3,10,5,6,2,5,9]
var origins = [2,2,1,2,1,1,1,2,1,1,1]
var fieldOfStudy = [6,1,3,1,2,3,4,1,2,3,3]

// 1,2,3,4,5,6,7,8,9,10
var commonEthnicity = [0,0,0,0,0,0,0,0,0,0]
var commonOrigins = [0,0]
var commonStudy = [0,0,0,0,0,0]

function machineLearning(ethnicity,origin,study){
    var placeholder;
  var i;
  for(i = 0; i < ethnicity.length; i++){
    commonEthnicity[ethnicity[i] - 1]++
  }
      for(i = 0; i < origin.length; i++){
      commonOrigins[(origin[i] < 2 ? 0 : 1)]++
  }
  for(i = 0; i < study.length; i++){
    commonStudy[study[i] - 1]++
  }

  placeholder = "It is likely that the next student will
be a " +
(commonEthnicity.indexOf(Math.max(...commonEthnicity)) +
```

```
1) + " with a " +
(commonOrigins.indexOf(Math.max(...commonOrigins)) + 1) +
" and they will study the field of " +
(commonStudy.indexOf(Math.max(...commonStudy)) + 1) + "."
 console.log(placeholder)
}

machineLearning(ethnicityArray,origins,fieldOfStudy);
```

So, if you picked this up and you're not too advanced into programming, this might look like gibberish so I will go ahead and break it down line-by-line. First up, we have our 3 "Tester Data" arrays, which is to say that it will be where we hold data for tests. The next three are what we will call "Semi-Persistent Results Data" and that means we will be shoving our results into these arrays so that we can keep score. Then we have our function with three parameters. I've hoisted the two variables, which is to say I setup two variables ahead of time so that it takes less steps when compiled as JavaScript already does this.

For our first for loop, I'm looping through the ethnicity array and this will give me a location inside of our SPRD, but I have to minus 1 to re-correct the position. Therefore, it would read as commonEthnicity[6], which would locate the "7" spot in commonEthnicity. The ++ at the end of that increases the value of whatever is in that spot, so since it is 0 then the 0 in the 7th spot in the commonEthnicity array would become 1. We iterate over the entire ethnicity array and tally up the different ethnicities. The third for loop does the same thing, but for the study set. The second one could also look like gibberish. You cannot set an equals sign in a ternary operator, but if that ternary operator is inside brackets then the final result can be used as an index. Therefore, for our first value of origins we have 2. This would then go into the operator and produce a 1 because it is not less than 2 and the new form factor this would take is commonStudy[1]++ and the ++ would just increment whatever was in that spot. Finally, I make a big string and use a combination of the Math.max function and the spread operator, which allows a programmer to find the max of an array in this situation. However, we don't want *just* the max, but the actual number. As an example, common origins would have calculated there would be more 1's than 2's so the Max would tell us that it would be a 7. Instead, we want to find the index of that Max number and add one in order to correct it back to the needed number so that we show that there are more 1's. All this and our program churns out:

```
It is likely that the next student will be a 5
with a 1 and they will study the field of 3.
```

This function is a complete "open and shut case" because we know exactly how many possibilities there are for each of the variables. The main variables will never change and thus we will never need any more than the empty arrays we have created to contain the result. We could easily double it like so:

```
var ethnicityArray =
[7,6,9,10,3,10,5,6,2,5,9,6,9,10,3,10,5,6,2,5,9]
var origins =
[2,2,1,2,1,1,1,2,1,1,1,2,1,2,1,1,1,2,1,1,1]
var fieldOfStudy =
[6,1,3,1,2,3,4,1,2,3,3,1,3,1,2,3,4,1,2,3,3]
```

This will still produce a result:

> It is likely that the next student will be a 5 with a 1 and they will study the field of 3.

This is still not machine learning algorithm though because while it did predict what the next student would be, it does not have the third part of nearly all machine learning algorithms and it has no way of learning from its mistake. The third part of a machine learning algorithm is the "Confidence Level" or better known as the attempt to estimate how sure it is that it got the right answer. When a machine makes a prediction, there's a certain percentage that this information will be correct. I suppose you could say that I am being unfair here because I've handed the machine a situation in which no matter how many times it predicts an answer, it will have no way of knowing why it got an answer correct or incorrect. However, this is because we are dealing with a very small data set and the numbers are calculatedly randomized. If we were to work with actual data sets with real humans being represented by those numbers, this would tell a very different tale. It is very important to think through the code or do a small section by hand to see if the machine will be able to accurately predict the needed result. Let's go ahead and create massive scopes of data for our machine. That's right, what was written here has the potential to become a machine learning algorithm. In order to do this, we're going to set up a three-year school based on percentages. Let's go on to the next section to begin diving into the second stage of developing a machine that can learn: Supervised Machine Learning.

SUPERVISED MACHINE LEARNING ALGORITHMS

Supervised machine learning algorithms are basically machine learning algorithms where you give the machine a helping hand in the beginning. These usually lead to unsupervised machine learning or even reinforced machine learning. Whenever you perform supervised machine learning, you are handing the machine the data sets and setting it up so that they get the right answer almost all the time. Once they get an incorrect answer, you then have to go back and see why it got the incorrect answer. Supervised machine learning is the first stage to almost all forms of machine learning because you have to watch and ensure that what is coming out will be correct or mostly accurate when you don't watch it or help it. This is why we need to change our algorithm to handle large sets of data that will have a helping hand in creating bias. Essentially, what we are going to do here is we are going to hand the machine learning algorithm (that we've partially created) the most biased answer we can possibly give it. However, we first have to rewrite our algorithm to handle years as one chunk of data. It is unlikely that students would have their ethnicity held in one database and their field of study in another database, so we need to change our algorithm to handle a multidimensional array.

```
var yearOne =[[][][]]
var yearTwo =[[][][]]
var yearThree =[[][][]]

// 1,2,3,4,5,6,7,8,9,10
var commonEthnicity = [0,0,0,0,0,0,0,0,0,0]
var commonOrigins = [0,0]
var commonStudy = [0,0,0,0,0,0]

function machineLearning(year){
  var ethnicity = year[0]
  var origin = year[1]
  var study = year[2]
```

Now that we have set it up to handle multidimensional arrays, we need to create a bias in the data. The usual method for doing this is to make the first data set completely biased, the second data set partially biased, and the last data set with only a slight bias. This gives the machine a starting point and then slowly balances the bias out so that when it hits random numbers, it's able to possibly make some more accurate guesses. In reality, you would have a large database where you would use testing sets to test your algorithm and once your algorithm showed promise, you would use the testing data instead of the multidimensional arrays we'll be using here. Then you would use your algorithm on the remaining amount of data to reap the benefits of non-simulated machine learning. Let's lay some ground rules for our experiment:

1. The end of the third testing stage will be a 2, 1, and 4

2. Each year will hold 50 students

3. The last year will be randomized but also doctored to provide bias.

Now, here is what the first year looks like:

```
var yearOne
=[[2,2,2,2,2,2,2,2,2,2,2,2,2,2,2,2,2,2,2,2,2,2,2,2
,2,2,2,2,2,2,2,2,2,2,2,2,2,2,2,2,2,2,2,2,2,2,2,2,2
,2],[1,1,1,1,1,1,1,1,1,1,1,1,1,1,1,1,1,1,1,1,1,1,1
,1,1,1,1,1,1,1,1,1,1,1,1,1,1,1,1,1,1,1,1,1,1,1,1,1
,1,1],[4,4,4,4,4,4,4,4,4,4,4,4,4,4,4,4,4,4,4,4,4,4
,4,4,4,4,4,4,4,4,4,4,4,4,4,4,4,4,4,4,4,4,4,4,4,4,4
,4,4,4]]
var yearTwo =[[],[],[]]
var yearThree =[[],[],[]]
```

And this is our result:

```
It is likely that the next student will be a
2 with a 1 and they will study the field of
4.
```

As expected, we have a completely biased answer. Now we need a multidimensional array that's only partially biased. Let's say our partial will be 50%. This is what the addition of the second year looks like:

```
var yearOne
=[[2,2,2,2,2,2,2,2,2,2,2,2,2,2,2,2,2,2,2,2,2,2,2,2,2
,2,2,2,2,2,2,2,2,2,2,2,2,2,2,2,2,2,2,2,2,2,2,2,2,2
,2],[1,1,1,1,1,1,1,1,1,1,1,1,1,1,1,1,1,1,1,1,1,1,1
,1,1,1,1,1,1,1,1,1,1,1,1,1,1,1,1,1,1,1,1,1,1,1,1,1
,1,1],[4,4,4,4,4,4,4,4,4,4,4,4,4,4,4,4,4,4,4,4,4,4
,4,4,4,4,4,4,4,4,4,4,4,4,4,4,4,4,4,4,4,4,4,4,4,4,4
,4,4,4]]
var yearTwo
=[[2,2,2,10,2,7,2,5,2,3,2,9,2,10,2,1,2,5,2,3,2,10,
2,1,2,10,2,7,2,5,2,8,2,4,2,8,2,4,2,2,2,6,2,6,2,4,2
,2,2,4],[2,1,2,1,2,1,2,1,2,1,2,1,2,1,2,1,2,1,2,1,2
,1,2,1,2,1,2,1,2,1,2,1,2,1,2,1,2,1,2,1,2,1,2,1,2,1
,2,1,2,1],[4,2,4,6,4,5,4,2,4,4,4,6,4,4,4,4,4,2,4,6
,4,6,4,6,4,5,4,6,4,4,4,5,4,4,4,2,4,4,4,2,4,4,4,6,4
,4,4,5,4,6]]
var yearThree =[[],[],[]]
```

And this is our result:

```
It is likely that the next student will be a 2
with a 1 and they will study the field of 4.
```

45

As you can see, our numbers have changed very little in between the years. Now it is time for the last year and only 10% of it will be biased.

```
var yearOne
=[[2,2,2,2,2,2,2,2,2,2,2,2,2,2,2,2,2,2,2,2,2,2,2,2,2
,2,2,2,2,2,2,2,2,2,2,2,2,2,2,2,2,2,2,2,2,2,2,2,2,2,2
,2],[1,1,1,1,1,1,1,1,1,1,1,1,1,1,1,1,1,1,1,1,1,1,1,1,1
,1,1,1,1,1,1,1,1,1,1,1,1,1,1,1,1,1,1,1,1,1,1,1,1,1,1
,1,1],[4,4,4,4,4,4,4,4,4,4,4,4,4,4,4,4,4,4,4,4,4,4,4
,4,4,4,4,4,4,4,4,4,4,4,4,4,4,4,4,4,4,4,4,4,4,4,4,4,4
,4,4,4]]
var yearTwo
=[[2,2,2,10,2,7,2,5,2,3,2,9,2,10,2,1,2,5,2,3,2,10,
2,1,2,10,2,7,2,5,2,8,2,4,2,8,2,4,2,2,2,6,2,6,2,4,2
,2,2,4],[2,1,2,1,2,1,2,1,2,1,2,1,2,1,2,1,2,1,2,1,2
,1,2,1,2,1,2,1,2,1,2,1,2,1,2,1,2,1,2,1,2,1,2,1,2,1
,2,1,2,1],[4,2,4,6,4,5,4,2,4,4,4,6,4,4,4,4,4,2,4,6
,4,6,4,6,4,5,4,6,4,4,4,5,4,4,4,2,4,4,4,2,4,4,4,6,4
,4,4,5,4,6]]
var yearThree
=[[2,3,6,1,3,2,3,10,7,10,2,8,6,7,8,2,9,3,3,7,2,3,9
,6,4,2,3,8,6,8,2,4,7,2,9,2,9,1,9,6,2,4,6,10,4,2,7,
10,1,1],[1,2,2,2,1,1,1,2,2,1,1,2,1,1,1,1,1,1,2,2,1
,2,1,1,2,1,1,2,2,1,1,1,1,1,1,1,2,1,1,1,1,1,2,1,1
,2,2,2,1],[4,6,4,2,5,4,1,3,6,4,4,4,6,4,2,4,2,6,2,1
,4,1,6,3,5,4,4,1,2,2,4,4,6,3,3,4,2,5,6,3,4,2,6,5,6
,4,2,6,6,6]]
```

And this is our result:

```
It is likely that the next student will be a 2
with a 1 and they will study the field of 4.
```

46

Alright, so even with a bias of 10%, we can still clearly see that we are getting the results that we want. However, we're still missing two very important components: Confidence level and Final Test. In order to figure out the confidence level, we need to be able to calculate the percentage of each category and then combine those into a single percentage. Since we chose an easy sample party of 50, this means we just double the number to 100 and the number itself. For instance, if there were 14 1's out of 50, we would say that there is a 28% confidence there is going to be a 1. Therefore, after some rearranging and rewriting, our code looks like this.

```
function machineLearning(year){
    var ethnicity = year[0]
  var origin = year[1]
  var study = year[2]
  var commonEthReal, commonOrReal, commonStReal;
  var commonEthPt, commonOrPt, commonStPt;
  var confidence;
    var placeholder;
  var i;
  for(i = 0; i < ethnicity.length; i++){
    commonEthnicity[ethnicity[i] - 1]++
  }
```

```
commonEthPt = Math.max(...commonEthnicity)
commonEthReal =
commonEthnicity.indexOf(commonEthPt) + 1
    for(i = 0; i < origin.length; i++){
    commonOrigins[(origin[i] < 2 ? 0 : 1)]++
}
commonOrPt = Math.max(...commonOrigins)
commonOrReal = commonOrigins.indexOf(commonOrPt)
+ 1
for(i = 0; i < study.length; i++){
    commonStudy[study[i] - 1]++
}
commonStPt = Math.max(...commonStudy)
commonStReal = commonStudy.indexOf(commonStPt) +
1
confidence = ((commonEthPt + commonOrPt +
commonStPt) / 3)
placeholder = "It is likely that the next student
will be a " + (commonEthReal) + " with a " +
(commonOrReal) + " and they will study the field
of " + (commonStReal) + ". I am " + confidence +
"% sure that this will happen."
console.log(placeholder)
}
```

This looks very nice and now when we run it on the 50% biased year, we receive this:

```
It is likely that the next student will be a 2
with a 1 and they will study the field of 4. I am
50% sure that this will happen.
```

As you can see, the confidence level is exactly 50% sure of this. Let's see what happens with year 2 and 3.

```
It is likely that the next student will be a 2
with a 1 and they will study the field of 4. I am
28.666666666666668% sure that this will happen.
It is likely that the next student will be a 2
with a 1 and they will study the field of 4. I am
20% sure that this will happen.
```

Those are some extremely intriguing results, but we're still not quite done because now we have to make it so that the previous year of data affects the confidence it has in the next year. This means that the equation either has to run in a loop or it has to accept whatever giant dataset we give it. Since a loop achieves both, we're going to have to reduce our years down into a single variable and then change our function so that it can run off that variable. Alright, so I've changed the years into one year and I've changed the algorithm so that it will handle as many datasets as we can give it. The results are astonishing. Here is the current code for the loop:

```
for(var i = 0; i < years.length; i++){
    machineLearning(years[i])
}
```

And these are the results

```
It is likely that the next student will be a 2
with a 1 and they will study the field of 4. I am
50% sure that this will happen.
It is likely that the next student will be a 2
with a 1 and they will study the field of 4. I am
78.66666666666667% sure that this will happen.
It is likely that the next student will be a 2
with a 1 and they will study the field of 4. I am
98.66666666666667% sure that this will happen.
```

You see, there's a small problem with our algorithm. It keeps collecting
the value outside of our function and so as long as no other number
increases more than our biased numbers then the percentage will never
go down. Additionally, there's nothing to take away that confidence if
the machine is wrong. Thus, we need to create an algorithm that not
only stores the prediction, but also loses confidence if it is wrong and
gains confidence if it is right. By simply moving those three variables

inside the function, we get a very similar answer when we tested them

separately. Here they are, inside the function:

```
function machineLearning(year){
        var commonEthnicity = [0,0,0,0,0,0,0,0,0,0]
        var commonOrigins = [0,0]
        var commonStudy = [0,0,0,0,0,0]
```

And here are the results because of the change

```
It is likely that the next student will be a 2 with
a 1 and they will study the field of 4. I am 50%
sure that this will happen.
It is likely that the next student will be a 2 with
a 1 and they will study the field of 4. I am
28.666666666666668% sure that this will happen.
It is likely that the next student will be a 2 with
a 1 and they will study the field of 4. I am 20%
sure that this will happen.
```

As you can, very similar results. What I am going to do next will make

some programmers cringe, but this is because I am taking a shortcut so

that you can learn how this would be handled. The next time this

function runs, it needs to know that a prediction was made. Then it

needs to check the first combination of numbers to see if it is correct. If it is incorrect, the algorithm would *normally* have to review why it was incorrect. On top of figuring out why it didn't work, it would also need to reorganize in order to develop a new prediction. Writing that part of the application takes months to years, thus I will be taking a shortcut by simply dividing the percentage in half every time it is wrong and then passing over half to the next equation if it is correct and not 100% confident. Also, we have to switch to recursion for loops inside of JavaScript because it can create odd issues when trying to grab values outside of the loop scope. Here is what that code looks like:

```javascript
var prediction = false;
var predictionSet = [];
var predictionTest = [];
var passover = 0;
var predictionResult = "";
function
machineLearning(year,prediction,predictionSet,pass
over, start){
        var recursionDepth = year.length - 1
        var commonEthnicity = [0,0,0,0,0,0,0,0,0,0]
        var commonOrigins = [0,0]
        var commonStudy = [0,0,0,0,0,0]
        var ethnicity = year[0]
    var origin = year[1]
    var study = year[2]
    var commonEthReal, commonOrReal, commonStReal;
    var commonEthPt, commonOrPt, commonStPt;
```

```javascript
 var confidence;
     var placeholder;
 var i;
 for(i = 0; i < ethnicity.length; i++){
     predictionTest[0] = ethnicity[0]
   commonEthnicity[ethnicity[i] - 1]++
 }
 commonEthPt = Math.max(...commonEthnicity)
 commonEthReal =
commonEthnicity.indexOf(commonEthPt) + 1
     for(i = 0; i < origin.length; i++){
     predictionTest[1] = origin[1]
     commonOrigins[(origin[i] < 2 ? 0 : 1)]++
 }
 commonOrPt = Math.max(...commonOrigins)
 commonOrReal = commonOrigins.indexOf(commonOrPt)
+ 1
 for(i = 0; i < study.length; i++){
     predictionTest[2] = study[2]
   commonStudy[study[i] - 1]++
 }
 commonStPt = Math.max(...commonStudy)
 commonStReal = commonStudy.indexOf(commonStPt) +
1

 if(prediction){
     if(predictionSet[0] === predictionTest[0] &&
predictionSet[1] === predictionTest[1] &&
predictionSet[2] === predictionTest[2]){
     var original = ((commonEthPt + commonOrPt +
commonStPt) / 3)
     confidence = (passover + original) >= 100?
passover + original : original;
     predictionResult = " Succeeded!"
   }else{
     var original = ((commonEthPt + commonOrPt +
commonStPt) / 3)
```

```
        confidence = Math.round(original/2)
        predictionResult = " Failed!"
    }
 }else{
        confidence = ((commonEthPt + commonOrPt +
commonStPt) / 3)
    passover = Math.round(confidence / 2)
    predictionResult = " There was no prediction
for this round."
 }
 predictionSet =
[commonEthReal,commonOrReal,commonStReal]
 placeholder = "It is likely that the next student
will be a " + (commonEthReal) + " with a " +
(commonOrReal) + " and they will study the field
of " + (commonStReal) + ". I am " + confidence +
"% sure that this will happen."
 console.log("Did the prediction come true?" +
predictionResult)
 console.log(placeholder)
 if(start >= recursionDepth){
        console.log("Analysis complete.")
 }else{
        prediction = true
    start += 1
    machineLearning(years[start], prediction,
predictionSet, passover, start)
 }
}
machineLearning(years[0], prediction,
predictionSet, passover, 0)
```

Let's go ahead and bring up our past results:

```
It is likely that the next student will be a 2
```

```
with a 1 and they will study the field of 4. I am
50% sure that this will happen.
It is likely that the next student will be a 2
with a 1 and they will study the field of 4. I am
28.666666666666668% sure that this will happen.
It is likely that the next student will be a 2
with a 1 and they will study the field of 4. I am
20% sure that this will happen.
```

And compare them to what our Actual learning machine tells us:

```
Did the prediction come true? There was no
prediction for this round.
It is likely that the next student will be a 2
with a 1 and they will study the field of 4. I am
50% sure that this will happen.
Did the prediction come true? Succeeded!
It is likely that the next student will be a 2
with a 1 and they will study the field of 4. I am
28.666666666666668% sure that this will happen.
Did the prediction come true? Failed!
It is likely that the next student will be a 2
with a 1 and they will study the field of 4. I am
10% sure that this will happen.
Analysis complete.
```

As you can see, we now have an algorithm that changes based on the results and gives us a different level of confidence in comparison to the biased results. Now that we have succeeded in making it to this step, we will now move on to Unsupervised Machine Learning.

UNSUPERVISED MACHINE LEARNING ALGORITHMS

Well, I suppose you could say that I fibbed about the Unsupervised part because this will be supervised. The primary difference between supervised and unsupervised is that the data set is known with the supervised version but the data set is not known inside of unsupervised and it's usually a cluster of data. Unsupervised learning usually handles various forms of classes rather than neat and organized arrays. For instance. Ethnicity would not be an array of numbers but, rather, a large selection of objects that belong to the Ethnicity class. Unsupervised is unorganized and you usually build a learning algorithm capable of organizing it on its own, but this would take thousands of lines of code and months of perfecting. Thus, we will go with the fibbed version to teach the lesson.

You see, the current algorithm has been changed to work with years and not monster. Monster is a huge array that I created specifically for this section and I'll tell you how I made it later on in this chapter. However, in order to understand why the difference between the two is a problem we first have to understand monster and how many levels it has as an array.

- You have the array of monster: []

- Then you have each element with the array of monster and this represents our years from year one to year ten: [[]]

- Within each of those years, you have three different categories, which leaves our final array looking like this: [[[],[],[]], [[],[],[]], [[],[],[]], [[],[],[]], [[],[],[]], [[],[],[]], [[],[],[]], [[],[],[]], [[],[],[]], [[],[],[]]]

- Up until this point, the most our machine has had to deal with is: [[[][][]],[[][][]], [[][][]]]

Therefore, when we reference each years, it goes years[0] for year 1 and then it follows after that. The good thing is that our years and our monster add up to be practically the same in terms of format, but our code will only process three consecutive years. In order for monster to work, we have to rewrite the code once more to look like this:

```
function
machineLearning(year,prediction,predictionSet,pass
over, start = 0){
  var refer = year[start]
  var recursionDepth = year.length - 1
  var commonEthnicity = [0,0,0,0,0,0,0,0,0,0]
  var commonOrigins = [0,0]
  var commonStudy = [0,0,0,0,0,0]
  var ethnicity = refer[0]
  var origin = refer[1]
  var study = refer[2]

      ...
```

```
    machineLearning(monster, prediction,
predictionSet, passover, start)
  }
}
machineLearning(monster, prediction,
predictionSet, passover)
```

This is what I mean by a supervised unsupervised machine. Unsupervised really just means that you run the machine without stopping it and see what numbers you come out with. If you were to run the previous code and just switch years[start] and years with monster[start] and monster, you would have only ever gotten three results like we had been getting with the previous testing data. This is because we were only expecting three results and when we got three results, it didn't seem suspicious. This is why there are two stages in testing for machine learning and why the second stage is almost always with a bigger data set, the bugs in your program become more pronounced. Imagine if we were a team of developers and we wanted to use this on all the students in the world. We would expect the prediction to take days if not weeks on a regular PC, but what would we come back to? We would come back to a program that spit out a bug because we didn't use an unsupervised testing batch. Now, if we switch it back to years, we still get our result:

```
Did the prediction come true? There was no
prediction for this round.
It is likely that the next student will be a 2
with a 1 and they will study the field of 4. I am
50% sure that this will happen.
Did the prediction come true? Succeeded!
It is likely that the next student will be a 2
with a 1 and they will study the field of 4. I am
28.666666666666668% sure that this will happen.
```

```
Did the prediction come true? Failed!
It is likely that the next student will be a 2
with a 1 and they will study the field of 4. I am
10% sure that this will happen.
Analysis complete.
```

This is almost exactly the same as our first results underneath the buggy

code, but when we run it with monster, it becomes:

```
Did the prediction come true? There was no
prediction for this round.
It is likely that the next student will be a 5
with a 2 and they will study the field of 6. I am
15.666666666666666% sure that this will happen.
Did the prediction come true? Failed!
It is likely that the next student will be a 2
with a 2 and they will study the field of 5. I am
8% sure that this will happen.
Did the prediction come true? Failed!
It is likely that the next student will be a 6
with a 2 and they will study the field of 5. I am
9% sure that this will happen.
Did the prediction come true? Failed!
It is likely that the next student will be a 7
with a 2 and they will study the field of 4. I am
9% sure that this will happen.
Did the prediction come true? Failed!
It is likely that the next student will be a 1
with a 2 and they will study the field of 4. I am
8% sure that this will happen.
Did the prediction come true? Failed!
It is likely that the next student will be a 2
```

```
with a 2 and they will study the field of 5. I am
9% sure that this will happen.
Did the prediction come true? Failed!
It is likely that the next student will be a 5
with a 1 and they will study the field of 5. I am
8% sure that this will happen.
Did the prediction come true? Failed!
It is likely that the next student will be a 4
with a 2 and they will study the field of 2. I am
9% sure that this will happen.
Did the prediction come true? Failed!
It is likely that the next student will be a 6
with a 2 and they will study the field of 3. I am
9% sure that this will happen.
Did the prediction come true? Failed!
It is likely that the next student will be a 9
with a 2 and they will study the field of 4. I am
9% sure that this will happen.
Analysis complete.
```

Now let's talk about the variable called monster. This is a multidimensional array containing 10 completely randomly generated arrays using this equation:

```
var empty = [];
for(var i = 0; i < 10; i++){
    var temp = []
 var one = []
 var two = []
 var three = []
 var j;
 for(j = 0; j < 50; j++){
    one[j] = (Math.floor(Math.random() * 10) +
```

```
1)
 }
 for(j = 0; j < 50; j++){
     two[j] = (((Math.random() * 10) + 1) < 5 ? 1
 : 2)
 }
 for(j = 0; j < 50; j++){
     three[j] = (Math.floor(Math.random() * 6) +
1)
 }
 temp[0] = one
 temp[1] = two
 temp[2] = three
 empty.push(temp)
}
document.getElementById("handler").innerHTML = "["
for(var k = 0; k < empty.length; k++){
     document.getElementById("handler").innerHTML
+= "[[" + empty[k][0] + "]," + "[" + empty[k][1] +
"]," + "[" + empty[k][2] + "]],";
 }
document.getElementById("handler").innerHTML +=
"]"
```

I am aware that there would be an extra comma at the end, but I was copy/pasting them so I didn't mind just deleting the small bug. This allowed me to generate an enormous amount of data that constitutes as 10 years' worth of data.

REINFORCED MACHINE LEARNING ALGORITHMS

Reinforced machine learning is when you have a machine try to produce results and then, basically, give them a true or false based on those results. You can actually think of this as reinforcing behavior inside of a child. Whenever your child does something that you don't want, they get a negative reinforcement so that they don't provide that result again. Likewise, positive reinforcement is when the child is praised or given something whenever they achieve an approved behavior. The truth of the matter is that machine learning follows a much similar path. The final stage of any machine learning is to let it loose on a final and much larger data set that is magnitudes larger than the original two sets of testing data, but the way we have developed this current algorithm has actually shown how reinforced machine learning is also a part of the creation process.

As we saw with our first bug, it produced an incorrect result when we were searching for something else. As a result, we changed the code and this gave us the result we wanted. This is not the reinforced learning that we are talking about. Physically changing the code does not mean that the act of you changing the code is reinforcement. Instead, it was when we decided to reward a correct prediction with an increased confidence and condemn an incorrect prediction with a decreased confidence that we incorporated reinforced learning. The expected result is rewarded while the unexpected result is often punished. This would normally prevent the machine from attempting to make incorrect predictions. As I mentioned when we first started with the code, the code is going to be extremely limited in scope. A normal learning machine is anywhere between 500-100,000 lines of code. It is simply impossible to make a learning machine that would fit into the pages of a book and not put limitations on it so that learning is not limited.

However, that does not mean that a machine learning algorithm must always utilize reinforced learning. Remember that reinforced learning is when it is possible to get the answer wrong and it requires that you be able to see that something can go wrong. There are somethings that one can get wrong even if they're geared to get it right and the data backs up their prediction. A good example is when a learning machine attempts to predict a stock rise or fall. The machine could look at all the stocks and point to which one rises and then point to the ones that will fall. The prediction could turn out wrong because of something that the researchers didn't put into the computer. This is kind of like children cursing when you least expect it but at a time when you would normally curse. Technically, the child was right about when they should curse but the parents did not account for the child being willing to curse. This can be negatively reinforced with the child, but a program will not see why it was wrong. The problem is that the issue is that of context and since the program was not taught context, it fails to include this into the prediction. It is an odd problem when a parent is the reason behind the child's misbehavior and the child didn't do anything it was told not to do but the parent has to deal with it now. In programming, the problem is compounded because context is usually not the goal of any machine learning unless there is a planned human element that needs to be involved in the process of prediction.

Let's look at a pseudocode example to help explain what reinforced learning is:

```
Start K(a,b)
Set up Repeat Cycle
Start b
 Repeat steps for b
    Choose a result (a) from the cycle of b set
forth by function K
    Use a to observe a new reaction call c inside
of b_special
    K(a,b) is K(a,b) + (maximum reward -
inaccuracies used to get to award +/- b_special)
    New b is created from b_special
 Do this until b no longer functions
```

As you can see from the pseudocode, a learning algorithm is quite simplistic by nature but as you can see from our code, it's complex by implementation. Essentially, when the program starts, you take a result from the current loop and use it to determine if a reward or punishment should occur. The loop then becomes recursive as a function, but it's recursive inside of a recursive. Even if one of the results becomes non-functional, the program will end that last loop and start the loop again from the beginning. It will run and rerun until the maximum reward has been achieved. Therefore, a much easier way to think of this is:

$$Result = AE = ASR$$

Result is equal to the multiplicative of Action and Environment. Environment is defined by the State of the program and its current Reward.

CONCLUSION

Welcome to the end of this book. What you saw here was a very basic version of machine learning. We did not use any outside library like Tensor Flow because that is a machine that had already been programmed. We would simply be learning how to use the API rather than learn all the different aspects of machine learning. By developing our own, small, and much buggier version you can learn how machine learning works, how it is developed, and what can go wrong with it. The first step to any machine learning is developing the necessary features for the machine to learn from. You can collect as many features as you want because the more features that your machine has to utilize, the more potential it has to be much faster during the learning process. However, be sure to check your parameters because redundant features and features that are not well defined can cause irreversible damage to the machine learning algorithm that are not meant to be shut off for a long time. The second step is to ensure that your algorithm follows the intended decision the design because any bug that you see will grow exponentially larger as your data sets become larger. Lastly, remember that machine learning is more about prediction not automation. As much as one may want machine learning to be for automation the end truth for machine learning is prediction. When you use machine learning for image recognition, it is predicting what the picture is. When you have machine learning drove a car, it is predicting hope a car should be driven. Machine Learning can be used to create automation but the machine is still predicting hope that automation should be carried out rather than always being 100% sure if it's decision. Keeping this understanding of the true end design of machine learning in mind will not only help you from making mistakes but will also help you refine the performance of your learning machine.

Before you leave, there are a few things I want to add that were not directly within the confinements of this book. While there is more than one type of machine learning, there is also more than one type of machine teaching. You are going to be the teacher of the machine and how you teach it really refines the answers that your student gives. Just as there are many different styles of teaching such as a lecture style or a visual style, there are more than a few ways to go about teaching your new machine how to provide the necessary results that you require. As an example, you already saw that we handed the picture an array of numbers, which would be classified as direct teaching. This means that instead of leaving the meaning of the numbers up to the program, we already know the meanings of the number and we just are seeking a specific solution from the program. However, if you look at something like Facebook's picture program, you will actually see that the picture program doesn't really have a point to it. Instead, the Facebook picture program is meant to facilitate various needs that one might have and the Facebook team have added needs on top of that. This would be called indirect teaching and it involves not giving a specific meaning to the action. This represents the two main ways of teaching your program, direct and indirect. Direct teaching means that you know the meaning of the data set and you might even give the program the meaning of the numbers if the program will find it useful. Indirect teaching means that you are handing the program a bunch of problems with a lot of goals but no end meaning as to what it's supposed to be doing. Facebook didn't really know why it wanted to incorporate machine learning into face recognition beyond the simple fact of identifying faces inside of pictures. It had a goal without any real meaning behind it and this is a much more difficult program to implement than saying that you want to identify terrorists inside of photos. By identifying just faces inside of pictures, you open up a door to many different additional features that the user can experience and use with the picture. The problem is that implementing machine learning without knowing why you're implementing it is going to be exponentially more difficult as well as exponentially more useful. It is essentially the end goal for most machine learning enthusiasts. While machine learning may have been invented more than a few decades ago, it is only been with in the past two decades that we've been able to put machine learning to any type of use. As we develop more and more complex processors and increase the power that our computers have, the more complex machine learning that our computers will be able to implement. Just as with education, this is the beginning of a new era and while this book may have gone over some of the current trends inside of machine learning, they can easily change over the next decade if you intend to stay in this science. This is a subject that is on the forefront of computer science right now and so you can expect that this will drastically change in the coming years, but as of right now we teach machines in very much the same way that we teach our own children.

Printed by BoD™ in Norderstedt, Germany